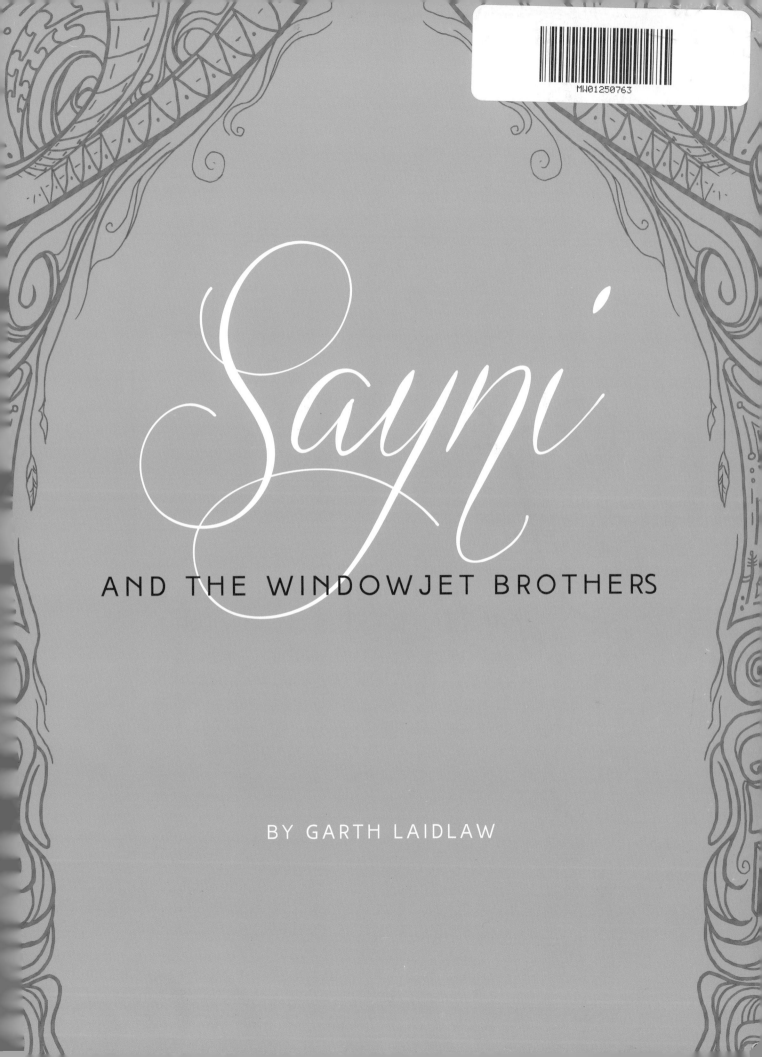

Sayni

AND THE WINDOWJET BROTHERS

BY GARTH LAIDLAW

There once was a town called Candleton that was built high in the sky among the clouds. The town was eternally lit by many candles that floated around it.

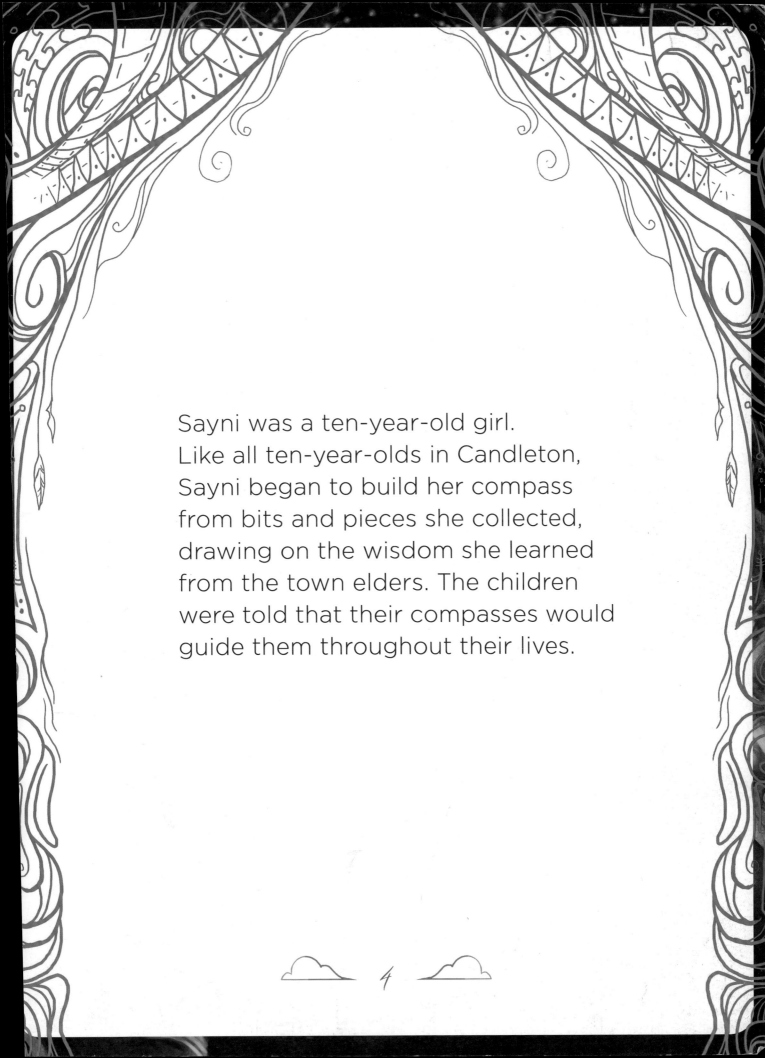

Sayni was a ten-year-old girl.
Like all ten-year-olds in Candleton,
Sayni began to build her compass
from bits and pieces she collected,
drawing on the wisdom she learned
from the town elders. The children
were told that their compasses would
guide them throughout their lives.

Sometimes, when she didn't know what parts she needed, Sayni would become sad. She would look at her compass, and see only an unfinished object. Why bother? she would think.

At times like this, she would visit her Uncle Garmo, and he would take her for long walks around Candleton. Together, they would discover fresh stories and hidden gems to add to Sayni's compass.

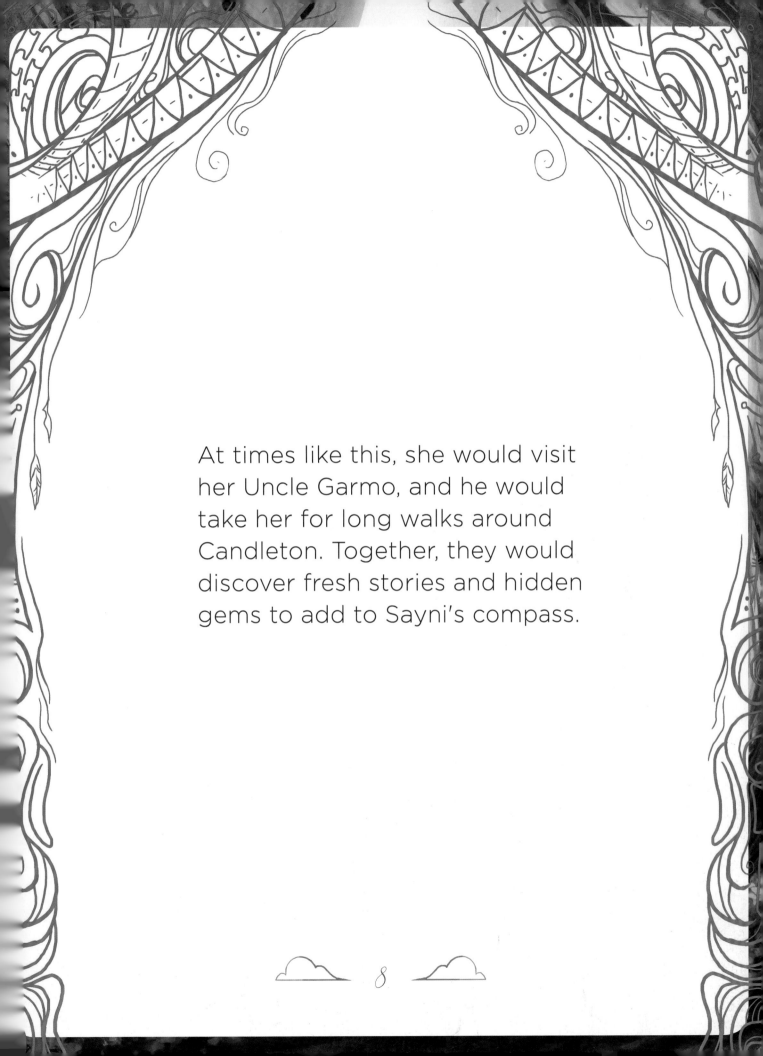

While she was out collecting alone one day, she came upon a strange sign that pointed off into an unfamiliar area of the town. Suddenly, and for the first time, her compass seemed to be pushing her in that direction.

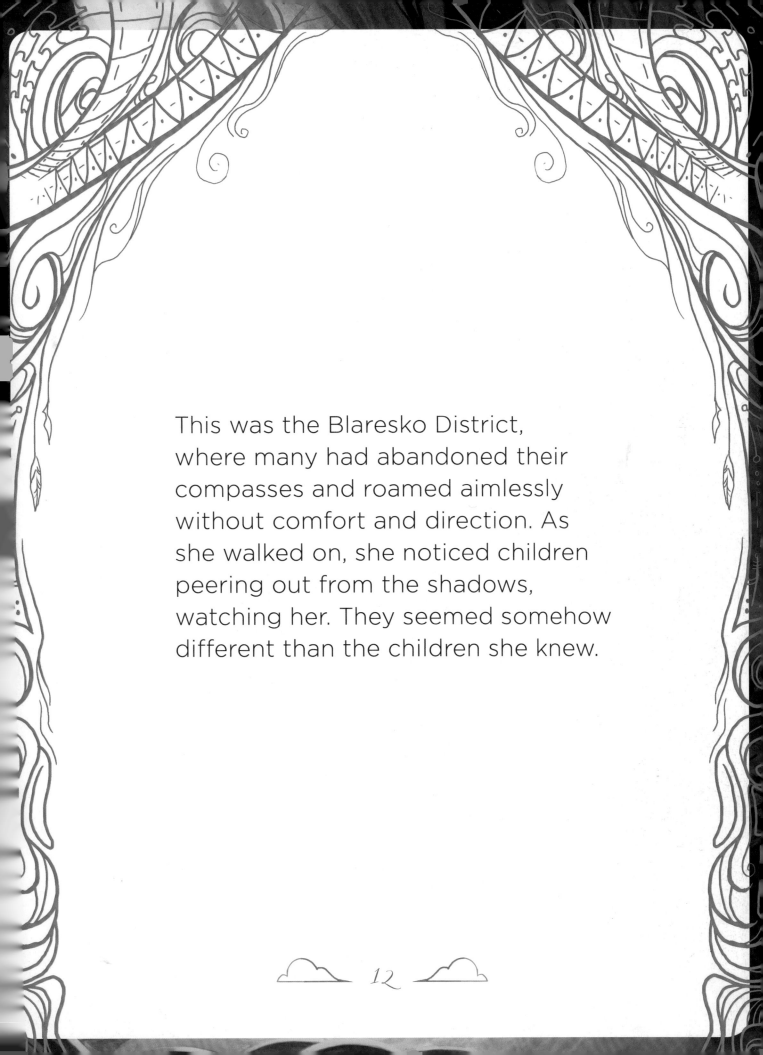

This was the Blaresko District, where many had abandoned their compasses and roamed aimlessly without comfort and direction. As she walked on, she noticed children peering out from the shadows, watching her. They seemed somehow different than the children she knew.

There were no candles adorning
the houses, no candles to light the
way. Sayni wanted desperately
to return to the warmth and light
of the Candleton she knew. She
turned a corner and discovered
there were large factories
beyond crumbling shacks.

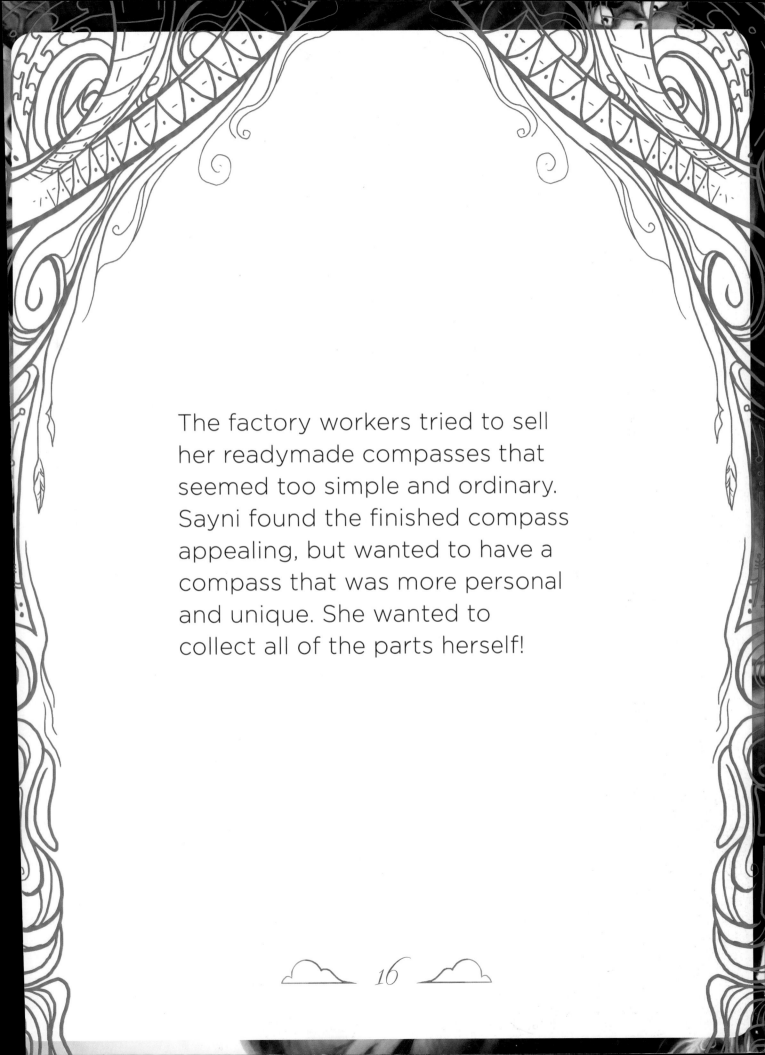

The factory workers tried to sell her readymade compasses that seemed too simple and ordinary. Sayni found the finished compass appealing, but wanted to have a compass that was more personal and unique. She wanted to collect all of the parts herself!

There were so many workers trying to sell compasses to her that she began to feel afraid. She ran until the night was so dark that she tripped and rolled down a grassy slope towards a large rock face.

Suddenly, the rock face seemed as if it was moving. Two small figures, made from rock and metal, appeared out of the rock. Sayni was dumbstruck!

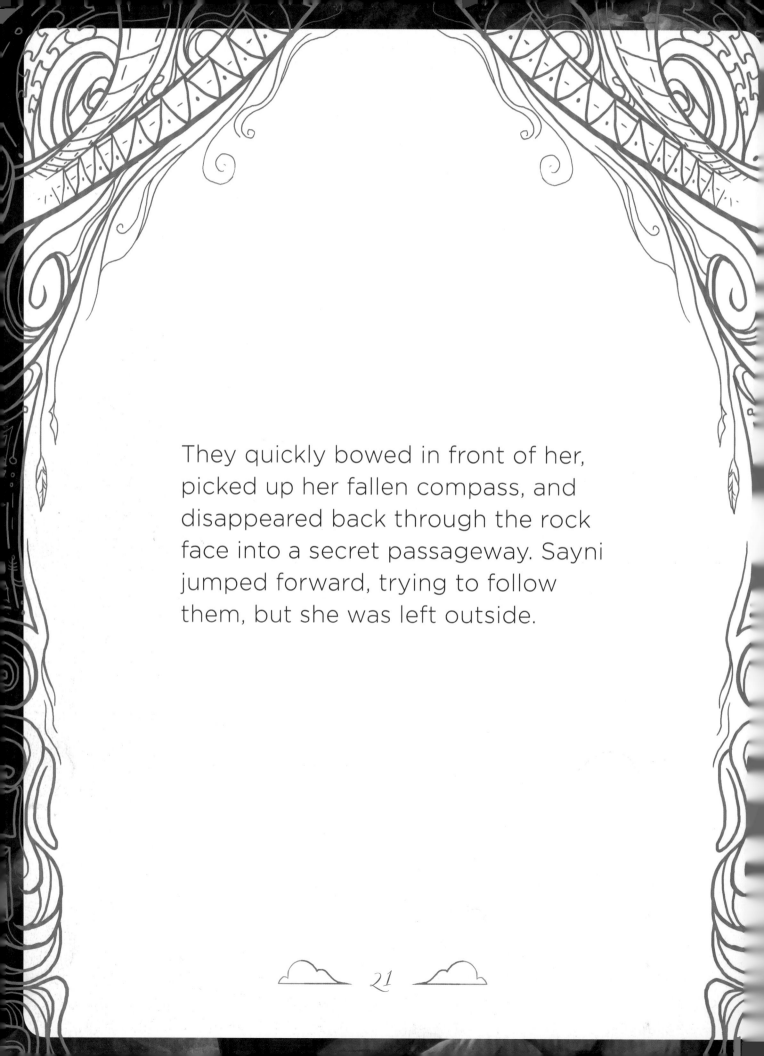

They quickly bowed in front of her, picked up her fallen compass, and disappeared back through the rock face into a secret passageway. Sayni jumped forward, trying to follow them, but she was left outside.

Sayni climbed up the rock face
and into a tree. She couldn't find
an entrance anywhere. By now,
she was very tired and eventually
fell asleep on a large branch.

When she awoke, she felt completely
lost without her compass. Suddenly,
a portal opened in the tree trunk,
and one of the tiny men emerged
to beckon her in. She was scared
but needed to find her compass,
so she followed him inside.

The secret passageway led to a busy underground workshop full of tiny figures who called themselves the Windowjet people. The two she had previously met were brothers named Polo and Appo. She spotted Appo working on her compass.

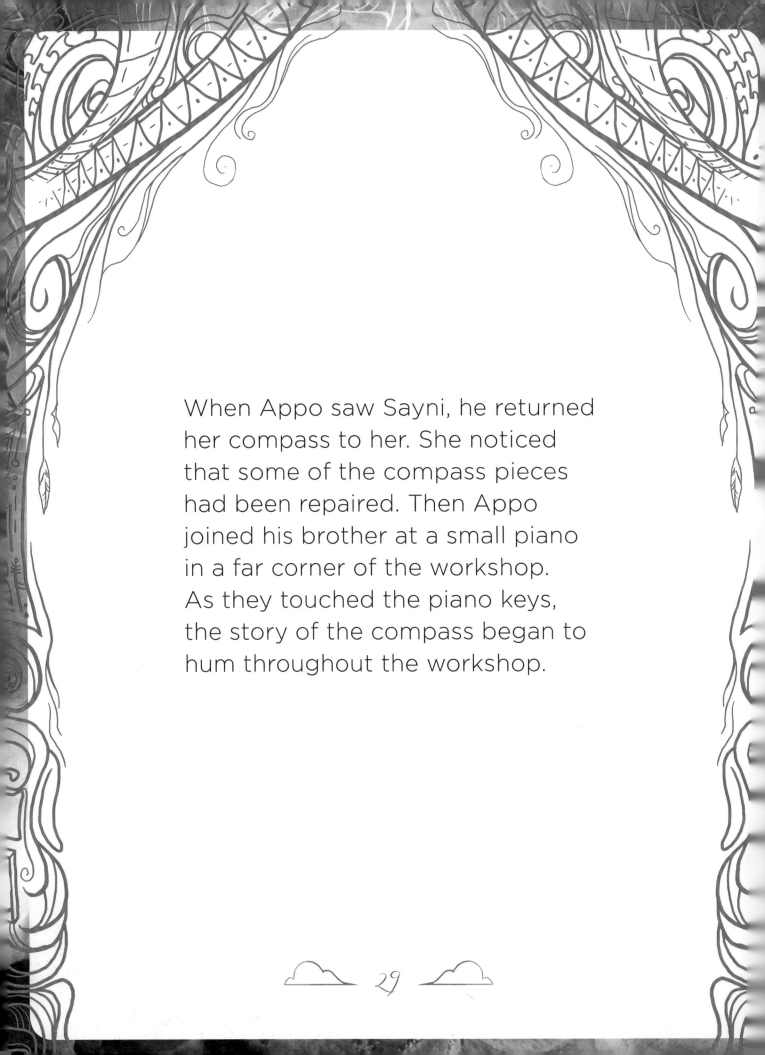

When Appo saw Sayni, he returned her compass to her. She noticed that some of the compass pieces had been repaired. Then Appo joined his brother at a small piano in a far corner of the workshop. As they touched the piano keys, the story of the compass began to hum throughout the workshop.

The song spoke of a time when all children had problems making their compasses. The Windowjet people helped them to recover their wisdom. All compasses could be unique, the story continued. The Windowjet people taught the children of Candleton that their compasses could guide them, and teach them who they could become.

As the humming ended, Polo and Appo bowed goodbye. Sayni found herself back in her own bedroom, looking down at her much-improved compass. She was so thankful for the Windowjet Brothers who reminded her of the importance of building her own compass. She only wished that fewer children abandoned their compasses.

For years afterwards, Sayni would teach the children of Candleton how to build their compasses from their memories, their friendships, and their love for each other. She taught them that a person's compass would, after all, guide them safely through the ups and downs of life.

◆ FriesenPress

Suite 300 - 990 Fort St
Victoria, BC, Canada, V8V 3K2
www.friesenpress.com

ISBN
978-1-4602-7696-9 (Hardcover)
978-1-4602-7697-6 (Paperback)
978-1-4602-7698-3 (eBook)

1. Education, Elementary

Distributed to the trade by The Ingram Book Company

Exercise

MAKE YOUR OWN COMPASS!

Get some paper and draw a big circle in the middle, taking up the whole page. Now, begin brainstorming all of the things that you love. Put these things in your circle. This collage will become your compass.

You can put anything in your compass. Words, quotes from others, pictures, even your favourite shoelace. If you like drawing, you could glue a pencil on your circle with one of your drawings. Be creative and arrange them in interesting ways. Try anything! Have fun with it!

Share this exercise with others! Your parents, teachers, or even between friends. Post a picture of it online with the tag #mylifecompass.

ABOUT THE AUTHOR

Garth Laidlaw lives in Guelph, Ontario where, among other things, he writes and illustrates stories. Garth is eternally curious, and tries his best to infuse his stories and illustrations with fragments of his own life experiences. In the future, he hopes that artists and storytellers will be sought after as leaders, because he believes that they can provide glimpses into a better world.

In order to defeat the almighty creative block, he takes long walks, listens to music, and always enjoys a good cup of tea. Aside from children's books, he also creates short animations and illustrates board games. Garth also teaches art, animation, and storytelling and runs weekly figure drawing sessions for his community. Find him on Patreon where you can help support his next project.

You can find Garth online at:
Facebook: **ArtStory** | Twitter: **@ArtStoryGuelph**
Instagram: **garth.laidlaw** | **www.artstoryguelph.com**

Printed in Canada

EVERY CHILD'S COMPASS MUST BE MADE VERY PRECISELY, AND EACH ONE IS UNIQUE.

FriesenPress

ISBN 9781460276976

90000 >

9 781460 276976

The Birth of Christ

STORICA